THE MOST INSPIRATI
FOR YOU!

15

AMAZING & INSPIRING

TRUE TALES

FROM MODERN HOCKEY GREATS

TERRENCE ARMSTRONG

CONTENTS

INTRODUCTION

Hockey is a universal sport, bringing players of many nations together on the ice. The stories of the legends of hockey will motivate you to never give up, and just might inspire you to pick up a hockey stick.

Don't ever let anyone tell you that you are not good enough. These players didn't give in. They all made it to the NHL, where they eventually became legends.

Here's a list of our heroes:

1. Sidney Crosby
2. Connor Hellebuyck
3. Mikko Rantanen
4. Artemi Panarin
5. Jason Robertson
6. Ilya Sorokin
7. Juuse Saros
8. Mitch Marner
9. Leon Draisaitl
10. David Pastrnak
11. Cale Makar
12. Matthew Tkachuk
13. Nathan MacKinnon
14. Auston Matthews
15. Connor McDavid

dryer so many times that it almost broke. It was dented in a hundred places, but somehow it kept chugging away and drying Sidney's hockey jerseys.

The first team Sidney played for was part of the Timbits Minor Hockey program. He quickly moved up the ranks until he was playing midget-level hockey at the age of 14—against 15- to 17-year-olds! He was already beginning to gain national recognition due to his impressive statistics on the ice.

Although he was a great player, he was still too young to play in the major juniors, which is a level between the minors and professional hockey in the NHL. Although his parents tried their best, the league's management would not agree to bend the rules.

Sidney decided to leave Cole Harbor to attend St. Mary Boarding School in Shattuck, US. This decision largely boiled down to the fact that he had lost the motivation to play for his hometown. Not everybody at home was happy with Sidney's popularity. In fact, it got so bad that people would call him nasty things from the stands and push him around on the ice. He finally decided that it was time to try somewhere else.

At St. Mary, Sidney met trainer Andy O'Brien, who helped him improve his game and made sure that he was always in excellent shape. Sidney worked with Andy three times per week. On other days, he would practice on his own.

Sidney's speed on the ice quickly improved, and his balance was top-notch. He set many scoring records at St. Mary, and even helped his team win the national championship in 2003. He eventually moved back to Canada to complete his high school education, and once he was done with high school at the age of 16, he was officially old enough to play in the Canadian Major Junior League.

INTRODUCTION

Hockey is a universal sport, bringing players of many nations together on the ice. The stories of the legends of hockey will motivate you to never give up, and just might inspire you to pick up a hockey stick.

Don't ever let anyone tell you that you are not good enough. These players didn't give in. They all made it to the NHL, where they eventually became legends.

Here's a list of our heroes:

1. Sidney Crosby
2. Connor Hellebuyck
3. Mikko Rantanen
4. Artemi Panarin
5. Jason Robertson
6. Ilya Sorokin
7. Juuse Saros
8. Mitch Marner
9. Leon Draisaitl
10. David Pastrnak
11. Cale Makar
12. Matthew Tkachuk
13. Nathan MacKinnon
14. Auston Matthews
15. Connor McDavid

SIDNEY CROSBY

Sidney Crosby is popularly referred to as the "Kid." But despite all of his wins and achievements at a very young age, he still remains humble and down to earth.

Sidney was born on August 7, 1987, in Nova Scotia, Canada—a country that is home to many famous hockey players. He grew up with hockey in his blood, and both his dad and mom had a strong connection to that sport. Sidney's mom had two brothers who played hockey. Meanwhile, his father was selected as a goaltender for the Montreal Canadians of the National Hockey League, but didn't end up playing for the team.

As a toddler, Sydney loved hockey so much that everyone would laugh when they saw the young boy clutching his baby bottle with one fat fist and a hockey stick with the other. He couldn't even walk yet, but he was already attached to a hockey stick! What a kid!

Sidney finally got his first chance to skate while he was three years old when he was given his first pair of skates and taken to the rink. He was a natural on the ice, and by the time he was five years old he was already playing better than many boys who were older than him. He had incredible motor skills that gave him an edge in the game.

Young Sidney loved hockey so much that his father painted the basement of their house to look like an ice hockey rink. He even set up a net so Sidney could pretend to take shots at goal. There was just one little problem: the clothes dryer. Flying pucks hit the dryer so many times that it almost broke. It was dented in a hundred places, but somehow it kept chugging away and drying Sidney's hockey jerseys.

The first team Sidney played for was part of the Timbits Minor Hockey program. He quickly moved up the ranks until he was playing midget-level hockey at the age of 14—against 15- to 17-year-olds! He was already beginning to gain national recognition due to his impressive statistics on the ice.

Although he was a great player, he was still too young to play in the major juniors, which is a level between the minors and professional hockey in the NHL. Although his parents tried their best, the league's management would not agree to bend the rules.

Sidney decided to leave Cole Harbor to attend St. Mary Boarding School in Shattuck, US. This decision largely boiled down to the fact that he had lost the motivation to play for his hometown. Not everybody at home was happy with Sidney's popularity. In fact, it got so bad that people would call him nasty things from the stands and push him around on the ice. He finally decided that it was time to try somewhere else.

At St. Mary, Sidney met trainer Andy O'Brien, who helped him improve his game and made sure that he was always in excellent shape. Sidney worked with Andy three times per week. On other days, he would practice on his own.

Sidney's speed on the ice quickly improved, and his balance was top-notch. He set many scoring records at St. Mary, and even helped his team win the national championship in 2003. He eventually moved back to Canada to complete his high school education, and once he was done with high school at the age of 16, he was officially old enough to play in the Canadian Major Junior League.

Sidney entered the Quebec Major Junior Hockey League (QMJHL) draft, and was the first overall pick! His reputation had preceded him, because the coaches of his new team, Oceanic, put him on the ice as soon as he joined the team. His first year in the major juniors earned him a spot on the Canadian Junior Hockey under-20 team at the World Junior Hockey Competition. This was the second time he would play here. The first time was after winning the title for St. Mary. Team Canada came in fourth overall that first year, but this time they came in second. During the event, he set the record for the youngest player to score a goal in tournament history.

In his 2003-2004 season with Oceanic, Sidney had a total of 54 goals and received the trophy for top scorer. He decided he was not going to go to college, and entered the NFL draft at the end of his second season.

Again, his reputation as an excellent hockey player preceded him, and he was once again the top pick overall—this time in the 2005 NHL draft. He was drafted by the Pittsburg Penguins that year, and began his NHL career with the team.

Sidney was chosen to play center for the team. To his great joy, his childhood idol, Mario Lemieux—whose picture hung on his bedroom wall—took Sidney under his wing. The Penguins star helped Sidney get used to playing in the NHL. He even allowed Sidney to live with him and his family during the season for the first couple of years of his career.

When asked how he felt about being in the big leagues, Sidney's response was, "It's going to be a challenge to go from junior to the NHL. I feel fortunate to be in this situation." Sidney clearly didn't take his position for granted. In his first season with the Penguins, he played hard and was named the alternate to the team captain. That was a big honor for an 18-year-old!

Before he had turned 20, he was officially the team captain, making him the youngest player to ever be named captain in the NHL. This was one of the biggest honors of Sidney's professional career.

Sidney dreamed of hoisting the Stanley Cup, and finally had the chance to make it happen in 2009, when the Penguins, under Sidney's command, made their way to the Stanley Cup finals. After years of trying and failing, the team had turned things around in the playoffs and made their way to the championship series, which they won!

Sidney's excellence on the ice wasn't limited to NHL play. On February 28, 2010, he scored the "Golden Goal" at the Olympics in Vancouver, Canada, where he was alternate captain for the gold medal Canadian team. Then, during the 2014 Olympic Games, he was named captain of the Canadian team. Under his capable leadership, Team Canada went on to win another gold medal in Sochi, Russia.

Over the years, Sidney Crosby has helped many children play hockey through his program called Little Penguins Learn to Play Hockey. He also cares a lot about sick children, having set up a foundation in 2009 to help them. The Sidney Crosby Foundation is based in Nova Scotia, Canada, where Sidney takes time to visit sick kids in Pittsburg- and Halifax-area hospitals. Not only does Sidney have two gold medals, but he also has a heart of gold!

FUN FACTS ABOUT SIDNEY CROSBY

1. Sidney loves chocolate chip cookies.
2. Sydney calls his mother before every one of his games.
3. Sidney is called "The Next One." This is a reference to him being the next best player after Wayne Gretzky, who is known as "The Great One."
4. His middle name is Patrick.
5. He has a program called Little Penguins Learn to Play Hockey to help children play hockey.

TRIVIA

1. Who was Sidney's childhood idol?
2. In the NHL 2005 draft, Sidney was picked by which team?
3. What part of Sidney's house was painted to look like an ice hockey rink?
4. Why did Sidney leave Cole Harbour?
5. At St. Mary, who trained Sidney and helped to improve his game?

INSPIRATIONAL FACTS ABOUT SIDNEY CROSBY

1. He was a good teammate and worked well with the other players.
2. He always wanted to improve his skills on the ice.
3. He made use of what he had to train himself, even practicing in his basement!
4. Even when others made fun of him, he was never discouraged.
5. He was dedicated to his team and always tried to inspire and motivate everyone around him.

CONNOR HELLEBUYCK

The goalie is one of the most important players on the ice. Being able to prevent the puck from sliding into the goal is a big task, and only the best and most focused athletes can excel in this role. Connor Hellebuyck was a legendary goalie who worked hard to become the best of the best while playing for the Winnipeg Jets.

Connor was born on May 19, 1993, in Commerce Township, Michigan. Hockey isn't as big of a sport in the US as it is in Canada, but Connor defied the odds to become an amazing, record-breaking hockey player from America.

According to his dad, Connor showed signs of being a goalie when he was just three or four years old. While watching hockey, he would always make sure he had on his "kit," which included a baseball glove in one hand and a mini-stick in the other. And even at this very young age, Connor was trying to mimic the goaltender! It was funny for everyone watching, because when the goaltender couldn't make a save, Connor would use his mini-stick and make the fake save.

Connor's dad also noticed how much he concentrated on everything around him. He would spot something, and his gaze would remain fixated on it for a while. Connor was developing the necessary skills for being a goalie without even being aware of what he was doing.

When he was four, Connor started road and roller hockey on the streets of Commerce, a Detroit suburb where he lived. Even in this game, Connor always had an interest in guarding the net.

When he was finally allowed to skate on ice at the age of five, Connor didn't let anything stop him from playing his favorite position. He eventually played goalie at Walled Lake Northern High School in Commerce Township, Michigan.

Because his parents wanted him to also have a social life while at school, and didn't want him to travel, he couldn't play at the level he aspired to, but on the bright side, this gave him time to pursue other hobbies, such as fishing.

After his junior year in high school, Connor wanted his dad to know how seriously he wanted to take his hockey career. He told his dad that he didn't have a backup plan for his NHL dream. His dad saw the determination in Connor's eyes, and that was when he knew that nothing would stop his son from playing in the NHL.

The summer before Connor's senior year, he developed his own personal style of goaltending. That summer, he got a new set of Reebok pads, which totally elevated his style of playing. According to Connor, these pads helped to form his playing style and the way he sat in the net.

Not only did Connor change his kit, but he also studied games. As if he didn't already have enough homework at school, he would watch hockey games and study goalies every chance he got. One lesson Connor quickly learned from all of the goalies he watched was how tense and desperate they became anytime they missed the puck. In response to this, Connor learned to remain calm and trust in himself.

This technique worked for Connor, and when he finished high school, it was what got him noticed by a scout for the Odessa Jackalopes. He was eventually invited to play for the Jackalopes in the North American Hockey League (NAHL) junior circuit.

Connor stood out at the Jackalopes' training camp, despite the fact that there were eight other goalies there, and eventually made the team. The Jackalopes made the playoffs, and he won NAHL goaltender of the year and rookie of the year.

Connor spent one year with the Jackalopes before he won a scholarship to play for the UMass Lowell River Hawks in the NCAA Men's Division—but he almost didn't get to play! The summer after his season with the Jackalopes, he decided to play roller hockey, like he usually did—but this time he tripped and crashed into the pavement. His arm began to bleed from the fall, and Connor began to cough up blood. His stomach hurt so bad that he retched on the floor. Luckily for him, there was someone nearby who called an ambulance, and he was rushed to the hospital. It was discovered that he had a ruptured spleen and needed emergency surgery to get it removed. At that point, his spleen had swollen to three times its size and he was bleeding internally. Fortunately, a surgeon was on site and able to operate on him immediately.

Connor was told that he needed two months to rest and recover, but he was back on the ice after one month. Connor played for the River Hawks for two seasons, and won the Hockey East Championship. He also made a Frozen Four appearance and was the only player in Hockey East history to be named tournament most valuable player twice! In addition, as the top goalkeeper in college hockey, he was awarded the inaugural Mike Richter Award.

Conner's dream came true on April 5, 2014, when he signed with the Winnipeg Jets of the NHL. He had made it to the big leagues! But he didn't get the chance to play until Ondřej Pavelec suffered an injury in a game against the Arizona Coyotes in November 2015. This was a chance that Connor didn't let go to waste. A week later, he won his first NHL game against the Minnesota Wild. A few months later, on December 27, 2015, Connor recorded his first NHL shutout in a win against the Pittsburgh

Penguins. From there, he went on to win many more honors and awards.

In his 2017-2018 season with the Jets, Connor set the record for most single-season wins by an American goaltender in the NHL. He also set a record for the most single-season home ice wins by an NHL goaltender. In April 2018, he was a Vezina Trophy finalist as the league's top goaltender.

On September 21, 2020, after years of being a finalist, Connor finally became the first goaltender in Winnipeg Jets/Atlanta Thrashers history to win the Vezina Trophy!

FUN FACTS ABOUT CONNOR HELLEBUYCK

1. Connor still uses Reebok pads today.
2. Connor is the co-author of two books published in 2023.
3. Connor loves ice fishing, and even designs masks based on the type of fish he hopes to catch.
4. He was born in Michigan.
5. He was the first goaltender in Winnipeg/Atlanta Thrashers history to win the Vezina Trophy.

TRIVIA

1. Where was Connor born?
2. How many years did Connor spend with the Odessa Jackalopes?
3. What year did Connor win the Vezina Trophy?
4. Connor got an invitation to play for what NHL team?
5. What position does Connor play for his team?

INSPIRATIONAL FACTS ABOUT CONNOR HELLEBUYCK

1. He learned from different sources, including studying goalies in hockey games.
2. He constantly skates to train, even during the offseason.
3. He always wanted to be a goalie, and never gave up on that dream.
4. He developed his skills and always stood out.
5. He loves being a goalkeeper.

MIKKO RANTANEN

We've all heard of famous players who don't like the spotlight, but who the spotlight has discovered nonetheless. Mikko Rantanen is a guy who likes to fly beneath the radar, but playing in the NHL as a winger for the Colorado Avalanche and scoring huge goals was bound to attract attention.

Mikko grew up with his parents and two sisters in Nousianen, a small town located north of Turku, Finland. He and his sister Laura were always best friends. They would play in the snow together and cook with one another. His mother loved taking them to a family-owned eatery called Restaurant Ask on special occasions.

Mikko's father would take him to the park to play games like soccer and baseball. When he was young, his parents wanted him to choose a sport. He enjoyed playing soccer and baseball, but those sports didn't truly excite him. He wanted to find the sport that was for him.

Right around that time, a brand new ice skating rink opened near their house. One day, after Mikko had finished his school work, his father took him to the skating rink. It had skating lessons for beginners, and Mikko's dad didn't hesitate to sign his son up.

Mikko practiced until skating became as easy as breathing for him. When the ice rink began hosting ice hockey games, Mikko's dad quickly signed him up for that, too. The coach, Aleksenteri, noticed Mikko's raw talent and saw a future star in the making. He took special interest in Mikko and taught him lots of important techniques, such as skating backward, hockey stops, and shooting.

Mikko loved skating so much that he would lug his skates to school and race off to the nearby skating rink as soon as classes were over. He had the encouragement of his parents, and worked hard to be the best he could be in whatever he did. His father only gave him one rule: to remain humble.

Mikko's first team was the Helsinki Knights. During their first game, Mikko scored a hat trick and led his team to win. Mikko scored three out of the five goals that his team earned that day, and the family celebrated his first win at Restaurant Ask, where Mikko ordered oven-roasted salmon. It's not every day you get your first win!

Mikko played very well in the peewee and junior hockey leagues, and eventually joined TPS of the Finnish Elite League, where he was allowed to play when he turned 16 years old. At that age, he was still skinny, but he was very fast. The coach noticed how fast Mikko was, but told him that he needed to build some muscles.

The young player began to work with Coach Hannu Rautala on building strength and muscles. This was a decision that would forever change his approach to hockey. Coach Hannu had a background in decathlon, and had spent years training different hockey players, so this was the right person to train Mikko. He created a series of workouts that were centered on building Mikko a new physique. He became huge, and could block with his body, giving his team a great advantage.

Another important part of his training was stretching. When he was young, Mikko learned stretching from his father—not the normal stretching we do when we wake up in the morning, but a full-blown stretching routine that lasted at least two hours! At night, after a day of playing hockey, he would sit in front of the TV and do his stretches. This was a practice he carried with him throughout his career.

Mikko's hard work paid off when, at 18 years old, he became an alternate captain for TPS. After spending a number of years under the radar, he was finally getting well-deserved attention from the international hockey world.

After TPS, Mikko was drafted by the Colorado Avalanche. He was also offered two athletic scholarships—one from Denver and the other from Harvard. He chose not to go to Harvard because he felt like he wouldn't be able to keep up with the academic requirements there.

When Mikko received the 10th overall pick in the 2015 NHL draft, it was a shock to everyone—including the Avalanche, who never expected that they would get Mikko on their team. He was such a good player, and his size and impressive skills on the ice were a great addition to their team.

When he arrived at the Avalanche's training camp, he impressed the coaches. They knew that they needed Mikko for the 2015-2016 season, and no one was surprised when they saw his name on the opening night roster.

While playing in the AHL, he was selected to the AHL All-Star Game. He was the second-youngest participant in this game's modern history. He was later selected for his second AHL All-Star Team, and shared the Dudley "Red" Garrett Memorial Award as the AHL's rookie of the year with Frank Vatrano!

When he returned to the Avalanche, Mikko was ready to go big. He scored his first NHL goal against the Winnipeg Jets, helping the Avs win the game. Then, on February 8, 2017, Mikko recorded his first NHL hat trick while playing against the Montreal Canadiens.

In June 2022, Mikko finally made it to the Stanley Cup finals with the Avalanche. They defeated the Tampa Bay Lightning in six games, and Mikko won his first Stanley Cup.

During the 2022-2023 season, he became the third Finnish hockey player to break the 50-goal mark in an NHL regular season, and the third player in the Colorado Avalanche history to do so.

One thing Mikko has never forgotten is how a new skating ring opening near his house gave him the opportunity to take hockey lessons and become a player in the NHL. Together with other Finnish-born hockey players, he has returned to Finland to donate hockey equipment to the community and support the next generation of hockey greats.

FUN FACTS ABOUT MIKKO RANTANEN

1. Mikko plays as the right winger of the Colorado Avalanche.
2. Mikko is 27 years old.
3. He played soccer and baseball when he was young, but knew they weren't the sports for him.
4. His first team was called the Helsinki Knights.
5. Mikko's favorite restaurant when he was young was Restaurant Ask.

TRIVIA

6. What was the name of Mikko's first team?
1. What was the name of Mikko's favorite restaurant when he was young?
2. At what age did Mikko become an alternate captain for the TPS?
3. Why did Mikko decide not to attend Harvard?
4. When did Mikko win his first Stanley Cup?

INSPIRATIONAL FACTS ABOUT MIKKO RANTANEN

1. He identified his weakness (his body size) and worked on it.
2. He wasn't afraid of hard work and lifting weights.
3. He is humble.
4. Mikko gave back to his community by donating hockey equipment.
5. He is very committed, even to stretching exercises.

I have included these free downloadable gifts to help light up your inner inspiration & reach your potential.

While you are reading through the stories, lessons and trivia, we recommend that you make use of all the bonuses we've attached here!

All our bonuses have been made specifically to help young athletes feel fired up, get inspired from the best to ever do it, and most importantly fall more in love with this incredible game!

Here's a list of what you're getting:

1) 250 Fun Facts From The World Of Sports
2) Sports Practice and Game Calendar
3) 5 Fun Exercise Drills for Kids
4) The BEST Advice From The Greatest Athletes Of All Time
5) The Mental Mindset Guided Meditation & Affirmation Collection
6) The Most Famous Events In Sports History And What They Can Teach Us

Now, it's over to you to scan the QR code, follow the instructions & get started!

ARTEMI PANARIN

From rags to glory, Artemi Penarin defied all odds. He was born poor and had to grow up with his grandparents. His first pair of skates came from a trashcan, and he wasn't even drafted into the NHL. But this is the story of how Artemi overcame the odds and eventually became a professional ice hockey winger and alternate captain for the New York Rangers in the NHL.

Artemi's childhood was pretty bleak. He was born on October 30, 1991, in Korkino, Russia, a place that was mainly home to miners. Just three months after his birth, his parents divorced and he was adopted by his grandparents.

Even though Artemi didn't grow up with his parents, his grandparents made him feel loved. His grandpa wanted him to play sports like the other kids, and, although they were poor, he managed to get Artemi a pair of skates when he turned five years old. But these first hockey skates were from the trash bin, and they were too big for him! He had to wear lots of socks, and sometimes his sneakers, to fit in them! His grandma sewed together jerseys for him to have something to wear to practice, and his hockey gloves were made from old gloves patched with leather from old boots.

Artemi's grandpa and grandma sacrificed a lot for Artemi to be able to play hockey. His grandpa had been a hockey player, and would spend time with Artemi, teaching him how to play. Artemi learned a lot from his grandpa, and when it was time for him to attend school, he joined the hockey team there.

Artemi attended the Traktor Ice Hockey School in Chelyabinsk. His grandma would sell milk from their only cow to buy gas for their old car so that Artemi could get to Chelyabinsk to play—six days a week, six months a year. Everybody had to be up early, and Artemi often slept the entire drive to hockey practice. Sometimes, the car would even break down when they were returning home after practice.

None of this stopped Artemi from playing his best, and soon, other parents began to notice. They would compare their children to Artemi, saying, "If only my son could play like that." It really made Artemi's grandparents proud to know that their sacrifice was paying off.

Artemi also played table tennis and other sports, but he mostly dedicated his time and energy to hockey. His grandpa made him do a lot of exercises. He would do squats to strengthen his legs, and always complain and groan, "Grandpa, my back hurts!" His grandpa's response was, "Don't worry, all will be great!"

When Artemi was 13 years old, he was suddenly cut from the junior club he played with in Chelyabinsk. Luckily for him, one of his friend's father found a boarding school called Podolsk in Moscow. The bus ride to his new school took two days, but when he arrived, Artemi received new equipment. He no longer had to play with holes in his gloves. It was the best thing that happened to Artemi that year.

When it came time for the 2010 NHL Entry Draft, Artemi believed he had the skills needed to play in the NHL. But no one selected him, and he ended the draft without a team. Rather than giving up, Artemi decided that he would make a name for himself wherever he got to play, even if he couldn't play in the NHL.

Artemi joined HC Vityaz in the Kontinental Hockey League (KHL). But the team was not impressed with Artemi's play, and three years later, they traded him for a draft pick—an undrafted player for a draft!

Artemi was traded to SKA St. Petersburg, where he recorded 26 goals in 54 games. He played an important role in helping SKA win the championship title, which finally got him noticed. He then signed a two-year contract with the NHL's Chicago Blackhawk and became one of the few players to make it into the NHL undrafted.

On October 7, 2015, Artemi scored his first NHL goal. It was also the first goal to be scored by the Blackhawks that season. The following February, Artemi scored his first NHL hat trick. He was finally making his name known in the NHL.

At the 2016 NHL Awards, Artemi was awarded the Calder Memorial Trophy as the NHL's top rookie. He was also awarded the Kharlamov Trophy by the Russian Hall of Fame as the best professional Russian hockey player.

In 2017, Artemi was traded again, this time for a pick in the 2018 NHL Draft. He ended up with the Columbus Blue Jackets. With this team, he set many new records, and even broke his own a few times.

The Blue Jackets defeated the New Jersey Devils in December 2017, when Artemi scored his second hat trick. That year, he scored 80 points in 80 games. That's an average of one point per game!

But Artemi was still not done. He signed with the New York Rangers, which was his final team. No more trading—he was finally home.

Artemi became the first Ranger to record 60 points in his first 43 games, surpassing the Rangers' most famous player, Wayne Gretzky. And he didn't stop here. He still had a lot to accomplish.

Artemi's greatest challenge was speaking English. For the past few years, he had a communication barrier since he couldn't speak English fluently. He's been taking English lessons on Skype, but it will still take a long time before he can freely converse in English. Luckily for him, his team understood this challenge and got him an interpreter for interviews.

In one of his interviews, he said, "It's tough, because I want to add a little bit of my own to the conversation, and I'm not quite there yet." Imagine having a lot of things you want to say, but no one understands you. We really hope Artemi learns English fast.

Artemi is known as a funny guy with a fun personality. He loves sharing things about his life on social media, where language is less of a barrier.

FUN FACTS ABOUT ARTEMI PANARIN

1. Artemi struggled with English and used an interpreter during interviews.
2. He is very active on Instagram, where he has over half a million followers and posts a lot about his travels.
3. Artemi's first pair of hockey skates were so big that he had to wear his sneakers inside of them.
4. He wasn't selected in the NHL Draft.
5. He set a record that surpassed teammate Wayne Gretzky.

TRIVIA

1. What position did Artemi play for the Blackhawks?
2. What happened in the 2010 NHL draft?
3. What exercise did Artemi do to strengthen his legs?
4. Artemi's first gloves were made from what?
5. What were the teams that Artemi played for in the NHL?

INSPIRATIONAL FACTS ABOUT ARTEMI PANARIN

1. He went from rags to glory.
2. He didn't grow up with his parents, but his grandparents showered him with lots of love.
3. He didn't have a lot of opportunity or equipment to play hockey.
4. He didn't get drafted into the NHL, but he didn't let that discourage him.
5. He was traded many times, but he finally found a home with the New York Rangers.

JASON ROBERTSON

Jason Robertson is the face of the Dallas Stars and the fourth player in the team's history to score 40 goals in a single season! He became one of the NHL's top offensive players at just 22 years old, and is one of the top scorers for his team.

Jason's father, Hugh, introduced him and his brother to hockey, and they were instantly hooked! They learned math by looking at the numbers on the back of players' jerseys, and learned to tell time from watching the clock counting down on the scoreboard.

When Jason was four years old, he began to play hockey under his father's coaching. A few years later, his family moved from Southern California to Northville, Michigan, to support their children's pursuit of the sport. There were better opportunities for Jason and his brother to skate in Michigan, and this was what his parents wanted for them. They would also buy tickets and go to the Plymouth Whalers games, which were played just a few minutes from their home.

Jason played for a number of different teams in Michigan. He played minor ice hockey for the Little Caesars, the Detroit Kings, and the Don Mills Flyers. In just one season with the Flyers, he scored 28 goals. He also got to play in the Ontario Hockey League (OHL) in 2015, where he competed for the cup. His team didn't win, but they placed second behind the Toronto Marlboros.

The young player then had to choose between being drafted by the Omaha Lancers of the United States Hockey League or playing in the OHL. He chose the OHL, and was immediately drafted by the Kingston Frontenacs. With his skills on the ice and natural instincts, he caught the attention of Coach Paul McFarland. At just 16 years of age, Jason was a starter for the team, making him the youngest person to ever play junior ice hockey!

In his first season with the team, Jason scored 18 goals. After two years, he became the first Frontenac to score 40 back-to-back goals in a season. He played on his team's offensive line and was named the OHL On the Run Player of the Week.

In the 2018-2019 season, he was traded to the Niagara IceDogs, where he helped his team win the Eddie Powers Memorial Trophy. He also won the Top Scorer Award.

Jason made his NHL debut in the 2019-2020 season with the Dallas Stars. He initially played with Dallas's AHL affiliate team, the Texas Stars. But after one season, he earned his spot on the Dallas Stars squad. In the 2021-2022 season, he had back-to-back hat tricks in two consecutive games. This earned him popularity in the NHL.

In the 2022-2023 season, he scored his 40th goal of the season while playing against the Flames. In doing so, he became the first player in franchise history to score 40 goals in back-to-back seasons. As Rick Bowness, former coach of the Dallas Stars, said, "He knows where to put the puck, he knows when to shoot it, where to put it. That's an instinct you can't teach. He's got it."

Jason had a series of ups and downs during his career, but he pushed on and remained determined. He still has more to accomplish in the NHL, and we'll be there to cheer him on.

FUN FACTS ABOUT
JASON ROBERTSON

1. Jason's mother is Filipino and his father is American.
2. He hosts a toy drive for children.
3. Jason's family moved to Michigan because they wanted their sons to play hockey.
4. He has three other siblings.
5. Jason has a brother who is also in the NHL.

TRIVIA

1. Who introduced Jason to hockey?
2. How did Jason learn to tell time?
3. How did Jason learn his numbers?
4. At what age did Jason begin to play hockey?
5. What team does Jason play for in the NHL?

INSPIRATIONAL FACTS ABOUT
JASON ROBERTSON

1. He chose to do something different. He didn't play basketball, but instead chose hockey.
2. He learned how to tell time and identify numbers through hockey.
3. He had really supportive parents, and his father taught him how to play hockey.
4. His parents relocated so their sons could play hockey.
5. He was hardworking and practiced skating during the offseason.

ILYA SOROKIN

Ilya was born on August 4, 1995, in Mezhdurechensk, Russia. His hometown had lots of mountains, and these became Ilya's training ground. His parents started teaching him how to skate when he two years old, and when he was five years old, they decided it was time for him to play hockey.

Ilya didn't always want to be a goalkeeper. When he was young, he wanted to be a forward, scoring goals. He started out as a forward for two years in the Russian youth leagues, but finally got in the net when he was seven years old. The first time Ilya decided to play goalkeeper, he allowed 13 goals. He doesn't even remember the final score!

Fortunately, Ilya's skills quickly improved. But first he had to overcome a few challenges. The biggest setback for Ilya when he was growing up was technology. His childhood goalie idols were Marc-Andre Fleury, Evgeni Nabokov, and Martin Brodeur, but the only way he could watch game highlights was on discs. Ilya had a disc of Don Cherry's highlights, and that was what he watched to learn how to play goalie.

In Russia, starting out in junior hockey requires you to join a team in the KHL or MHL. If your area doesn't have any of these teams, you might have to move to be able to play. Unfortunately for Ilya, his area had no KHL or MHL teams, so, at the age of 12, he moved to Novokuznetsk, a few hours from home.

Moving away from home is always hard—you miss home, your family, and your friends. Even if the move is for a good opportunity, sometimes you feel like running back to the familiarity of your hometown. Ilya experienced all of this, but instead of returning home, he stayed and made new friends—and as time went by, things became a bit easier.

Ilya's new friends made everything better, even when he had to endure long bus rides to games. He played 20-30 games per season, and his longest bus ride was 18-20 hours to Kazakhstan. But for Ilya, it was fun. "It was not bad for kids. It was a fun time," he said.

Ilya played with the local clubs until he was 17 years old. He then had the opportunity to play in the KHL. He joined Metallurg Novokuznetsk in 2012, and played there for three seasons before being traded to CSKA Moscow. This was the opportunity that Ilya needed to be noticed as an exemplary goalkeeper. He even won a Gagarin Cup in 2019 and was named the most valuable player of the 2019 Gagarin Cup playoffs.

Ilya finally got the chance to play in the NHL. He was drafted by the New York Islanders in the 2019 NHL draft, but he couldn't play due to the COVID-19 pandemic. Fortunately, by 2021, he was back on the ice. He was originally meant to be a backup for his first game, which was against the New York Rangers, but the starting goalkeeper had an injury and couldn't play, and Ilya got his big break. Unfortunately, the Islanders lost that game, but Ilya bounced back and practiced even harder.

His first NHL win was in February 2021, a year after his first appearance for the Islanders. This game was against the Buffalo Sabres. Ilya made 20 saves during the game, shutting out the Sabres. It was a perfect game!

In the 2022-2023 season, Ilya was a finalist for the Vezina Trophy, which is awarded to the league's best goaltender. His goalkeeping skills also helped the Islanders qualify for the Stanley Cup playoffs.

One major issue Ilya had when relocating to North America was the language barrier. He had to learn a new language, so, in addition to practicing on the ice, he also practiced English in his spare time.

ya's current goal is to learn English. To that end, he has been taking English classes since 2020.

FUN FACTS ABOUT
ILYA SOROKIN

1. Ilya moved away from home at the age of 12.
2. He learned about goalkeeping from a disc of Don Cherry highlights.
3. Ilya didn't want to be a goalkeeper when he was young.
4. He now plays for the New York Islanders of the NHL.
5. Ilya is godfather to Igor Sheterkin's son.

TRIVIA

1. What position does Ilya play for the New York Islanders?
2. What is Ilya's nationality?
3. Who are Ilya's best friends?
4. What position did Ilya play when he was four years old?
5. What did Ilya struggle with when he came to North America?

INSPIRATIONAL FACTS ABOUT
ILYA SOROKIN

1. He demonstrates a level of confidence that motivates his teammates.
2. He didn't let the language barrier discourage him from playing.
3. His determination made him stand out from his peers.
4. Ilya had only a disc of Don Cherry highlights, but he learned all he could from it.
5. He was not afraid to learn a new language.

JUUSE SAROS

Here is another story of a goalie who is one of the top 10 goalkeepers in the NHL. He is well on his way to becoming a legend in the hockey world.

Juuse Saros, popularly known as "Juice," was born on July 19, 1995, in Forssa, Finland. Juuse's family moved around when he was young because of his father's job. They moved from Forssa to Naantali when he was just three years old. Four years later, they moved again—this time to Hämeenlinna, where they stayed for just one year before moving back to Naantali.

After all of these moves, when Juuse was 10 years old, his family finally settled in Hämeenlinna. By this time, Juuse had discovered that he loved playing sports, including ice hockey, floorball, and soccer.

His first hockey team was part of the local neighborhood junior league. As a morale booster for the young kids, the teams were named after NHL teams. Juuse's first team was named after the Edmonton Oilers.

Juuse originally played as a defenseman, but when he was 13 years old, he switched to goaltender. From that point on, that was the only position he wanted to play. For Christmas, he even asked for a glove and a blocker!

When Juuse joined the HPK Hämeenlinna Juniors, there was a little bit of a problem: The team already had goalies, and they weren't interested in making Juuse a goaltender. Juuse told his father that he wasn't interested in playing hockey if he couldn't be a goalie. Finally, a compromise was reached—Juuse would play as goalie during practice sessions. This satisfied him. At least he had the opportunity to play his favorite position some of the time.

Playing hockey didn't stop Juuse from studying and graduating. In fact, his school was a specialized sports high school that allowed him to take morning classes so he could keep up with the classes that overlapped with his hockey practice. Juuse ended up graduating high school in three years!

He went on to play with the HPK U16 team, which consisted of players from Hameenlinna, Riihimaki, and Hyinkaa. While on the team, he met goalkeeping coach, Antti Meriläinen, and the two became friends. Juuse was like a sponge, ready to absorb all the knowledge he could about how he could play better. He even attended summer hockey camps, where he learned about the importance of stretching. Juuse took this practice to heart and would stretch for 15 minutes before breakfast every morning. He even stretched on Christmas day—that was how committed he was to his practice.

Juuse played in the HPK U16, U18 and U20, and he performed well as a goalkeeper. He was even named the best goaltender in the league when he was playing in the U16. Although Coach Lukkari noticed some flaws in his performance, he and Juuse worked hard to improve them.

Juuse became so good that he was selected to represent his homeland in international competition. He played for Finland at the 2012 Ivan Hlinka Memorial Tournament, where he helped his team win a silver medal.

When he returned home to the HPK, he took his position as the starting goaltender for the U20. He played hard, earning his team a spot in the playoffs and finishing the season with a bronze medal.

In 2012, playing goalkeeper became a chore for Juuse. He had lost the fun of playing hockey. He felt he was not meeting the high standards he had set for himself, and this made him unfocused.

Everyone gets down at some point, and we all need someone there to lift us up. Luckily for Juuse, he had Coach Lukkari. "We had to work to make playing more enjoyable again. He had to become more relaxed so he would be able to get his flow back," Lukkari said.

His plan worked, and Juuse was able to get back into the flow. He stopped measuring himself against unreasonably high standards and just did what he did best—guard the net. The newly focused Juuse played better than ever that year and led the HPK U20 to their very first championship!

During the 2012-2013 season, he was named to the Jr. A SM-Liiga All-Star Team and chosen as the best player in the league. He also received the Jorma Valtonen Award as the league's top goaltender.

Despite his many achievements, Juuse remained humble and modest. His coach even described him as too humble and too modest, as well as a bit nervous.

It was clear that Juuse was talented, but scouts were a bit worried about his height. He was only 5'10", which was considered too short for a goalkeeper. It even got to the point where some scouts had Juuse do a test to see if he would grow taller.

Despite this challenge, Juuse didn't give up on his dreams of playing in the NHL, and he was finally drafted by the Nashville Predators. He was actually picked on a whim. The Predators had only three picks, and they didn't even need a goalie. If Juuse had been just a few inches taller, he would have been picked instantly, but because of his height he was the 99th overall pick in the 2013 NHL Entry Draft.

After training camp, Juuse was assigned to the Milwaukee Admirals in the American Hockey League (AHL). He had this to say about North America: "There's much to learn for European goalies. The rink is smaller, and the style of play is different." Fortunately, he didn't let the different playing style stop him. He quickly adapted, and had an impressive rookie season. He was named to the AHL's All-Rookie Team and AHL All-Star Game.

Juuse began playing for the Predators in 2015, but as a backup for the Predators current goalkeeper, Pekka Rinne. In October 2016, Juuse notched his first NHL win against the Pittsburg Penguins, making 34 saves in that game. A few months later, he earned his first NHL shutout in December 2016.

During the 2017-2018 season, he set a Predators record for most saves in a game against the Edmonton Oilers. Because of this feat, he was named to the NHL All-Rookie team in 2017.

In July 2021, Juuse became the team's main goalie after Pekka retired. He led the Predators to the Stanley Cup playoffs in 2021, but they were eliminated by the Carolina Hurricanes in the first round. He was a finalist for the Vezina Trophy, which is given to the best goalie in the NHL.

Today, Juuse Saros, emerged as a hockey wizard for the Nashville Predators. Setting a record for saves in 2017, he joined the NHL All-Rookie team. In 2021, he became the main goalie, leading the Predators to the playoffs and earning a spot as a Vezina Trophy finalist. Juuse's journey promises a magical future, leaving an indelible mark on the Nashville Predators' enchanted history.

FUN FACTS ABOUT
JUUSE SAROS

1. Juuse was born in Finland.
2. He wanted to quit hockey because he discovered he might not be able to play as a goalie.
3. Juuse loved playing floorball and soccer when he was young.
4. His nickname is "Juice" because of how you pronounce his name.
5. Juuse asked for a glove and blocker for Christmas because he really wanted to play goalie.

TRIVIA

1. What position does Juuse play?
2. Why is Juuse's nickname Juice?
3. What team does Juuse play for?
4. What is Juuse's jersey number?
5. Where is Juuse from?

INSPIRATIONAL FACTS ABOUT
JUUSE SAROS

1. He knew what position he wanted to play when he started playing hockey.
2. Juuse made Predators history during the 2017-2018 season by setting a record for the most saves in a single game against the Edmonton Oilers, showcasing his extraordinary skill and resilience.
3. His height didn't stop Juuse's dream of being a goalie.
4. Having fun while playing hockey was very important to Juuse.
5. He was dedicated to practicing and training.

I have included these free downloadable gifts to help light up your inner inspiration & reach your potential.

While you are reading through the stories, lessons and trivia, we recommend that you make use of all the bonuses we've attached here!

All our bonuses have been made specifically to help young athletes feel fired up, get inspired from the best to ever do it, and most importantly fall more in love with this incredible game!

Here's a list of what you're getting:

1) 250 Fun Facts From The World Of Sports
2) Sports Practice and Game Calendar
3) 5 Fun Exercise Drills for Kids
4) The BEST Advice From The Greatest Athletes Of All Time
5) The Mental Mindset Guided Meditation & Affirmation Collection
6) The Most Famous Events In Sports History And What They Can Teach Us

Now, it's over to you to scan the QR code, follow the instructions & get started!

MITCH MARNER

Mitch Marner was born on May 5, 1997, in Markham, Ontario. When he was two, his father decided it was time to teach Mitch how to skate. A pond became their training ground, and Mitch was a natural.

Mitch's older brother played hockey, and this inspired him when he was a kid. Like most younger brothers, he wanted to be like his sibling.

Mitch learned how to skate through a Mini Blades program in Newcastle. His parents were obsessed with hockey, and he grew up as a Maple Leafs fan. Little did he know that he would one day end up playing on the team.

His first team was the Malvern Vipers, and he played for them for two years. They won a few tournaments, which was pretty amazing, since Mitch was only four years old.

At the age of six, he tried out for the Clarington Novice AAA team and scored more points than anyone else in the tryouts, but the coach decided that Mitch was too young to play. He wasn't mentally ready yet.

Mitch wasn't too happy about this, but he shrugged it off and decided to go to the Lindsay Wolves, where he played for their Novice AAA team and scored goals for the team.

When he was seven, he returned to Clarington and was accepted onto the team. The coach had finally decided he was old enough to play, and that season, young Mitch led the team. They won the OMHA silver medal thanks to the goals he scored.

The following year, due to age requirements, Mitch had to find a new team to play with. He moved to the Whitby Wildcats, where he once again scored a number of goals. He led the team to an OMHA silver medal, the second of his young career.

After playing for the Wildcats, Mitch played for the Vaughan Kings. He was so good that he had to play with kids who were older than him. Mitch was a great addition to the Kings. The team was struggling, but after Mitch joined, everything changed. The team jumped from 11th to 4th and made their way to the GTHL Championship in Peewee, where they won a GTHL title!

Mitch also played with the Don Mills Flyers. At the end of his season there, he was invited to join the St. Michael's Buzzers of the Ontario Junior A Hockey League.

Finally, it was time for college, and Mitch received a scholarship offer from the University of Michigan. At the same time, he was drafted by the London Knights in the 2013 OHL Priority Selection. It was a tough decision for Mitch. The University of Michigan had produced lots of players who were now in the NHL, but he decided to sign with the London Knights.

Mitch was selected in the first round and was the 19th overall pick. During his rookie season, he had 59 points in 64 games and was runner-up for the OHL Rookie of the Year.

His second year with the Knights, he was named to the OHL First All-Star Team and awarded the Jim Mahon Memorial Trophy. He was the OHL's highest-scoring right wing player, and this was what got him noticed in the NHL 2015 Draft.

Mitch eventually signed with the Toronto Maple Leafs, his favorite team as a child. That same year, he was named co-captain of the London Knights. The Knights ended the regular season as the highest scoring team in the OHL, all thanks to Mitch and the other wingers. In fact, he was awarded the Red Tilson Trophy as the OHL's most outstanding player of the year!

During the 2016 OHL playoffs, Mitch led his team to the championships, where they won. His spectacular performance in the playoffs won him the Wayne Gretzky 99 Award as the playoff's most valuable player.

After helping the Knights win the 2016 Memorial Cup, Mitch won the Stafford Smythe Memorial Trophy and the Ed Chynowett Trophy as tournament MVP and lead scorer. This made him the second OHL player (after Brad Richards in 2000) to win five awards in the same season.

In the 2017-2018 season, Mitch Marner showcased his brilliance on the ice for the Toronto Maple Leafs. During the Next Century Game, he recorded a remarkable four-point performance, contributing one goal and three assists to secure a victory against the Carolina Hurricanes. This wasn't the end of Mitch's magic in that season – he made Leafs history by becoming the first player to achieve five points in a single game.

The following year, in the 2018 Stanley Cup playoffs, Mitch continued to leave his mark as the first Leafs player with a five-game point streak. However, despite his efforts, the Maple Leafs were eliminated in the first round by the Boston Bruins.

Fast forward to the 2019-2020 season, Mitch Marner's leadership qualities were recognized as he was named an alternate captain for the Maple Leafs. In a memorable moment in December 2019, he orchestrated a comeback with a game-winning breakaway goal, showcasing his clutch play and determination. In the 2021-2022 season, Mitch's star continued to rise with an impressive record of 35 goals and 62 assists in 72 games.

His standout performance, including a four-goal, six-point game against the Detroit Red Wings, earned him a spot on the NHL First All-Star Team as the league's best right winger. Mitch Marner's journey with the Maple Leafs is a testament to his skill, leadership, and ability to make history on the ice.

FUN FACTS ABOUT
MITCH MARNER

1. When he is not playing hockey, Mitch likes to watch movies and play video games.
2. In the 2016-2017 season, Mitch broke the record for most assists in a season, which had stood for 73 years.
3. Mitch has always been a Maple Leafs fan, ever since he was a child.
4. He started a business in high school called The MOD Feast.
5. Mitch was the fourth overall selection in the first round of the 2015 NHL Draft.

TRIVIA

1. Where was Mitch Marner born?
2. What team does Mitch play for in the NHL?
3. In the 2015-2016 season with the Knights, Mitch won five awards in a single season. Can you name them?
4. What is Mitch's jersey number?
5. What position does Mitch play for his team?

INSPIRATIONAL FACTS ABOUT
MITCH MARNE

1. Marner's leadership qualities were acknowledged when he was named an alternate captain for the Toronto Maple Leafs during the 2019-2020 NHL season, inspiring teammates with his on-ice prowess and off-ice demeanor.
2. In December 2019, Marner orchestrated a memorable comeback for the Maple Leafs with a game-winning breakaway goal, showcasing his clutch performance and ability to shine in critical moments.

3. Mitch Marner is known for his philanthropic efforts, particularly his significant contributions to various charitable causes, embodying the spirit of giving back to the community.
4. Mitch made Leafs history during the 2017-2018 season by becoming the first player to record five points in a single game, demonstrating his exceptional skill and impact on the ice.
5. Marner's outstanding performance in the 2021-2022 season, recording 35 goals and 62 assists in 72 games, earned him a spot on the NHL First All-Star Team as the league's best right winger, inspiring aspiring players with his dedication and excellence.

LEON DRAISAITL

Leon Draisaitl is the first German player on our list. He has earned the nickname the "German Gretzky," and we will soon find out why!

Leon was born on October 27, 1995, in Cologne, Germany. His father, Peter Draisaitl, played ice hockey for the Kölner Haie of the Deutsche Eishockey Liga. He also played for the German national team in three Winter Olympics. Suffice to say, Leon grew up with a lot of knowledge about ice hockey!

Of course, just because his father was a hockey player didn't stop Leon from playing other sports. He played soccer, ice hockey, tennis, and even golf. But he eventually discovered that he preferred the puck to the ball, and stuck with ice hockey, just like his father.

Leon's father coached him during his childhood. This was a great bonding experience for the two of them, and also equipped Leon with the skills that he needed to thrive as a player.

As a teen, Leon played ice hockey with the Kölner Haie under-16 and the Adler Mannheim under-18 teams. His father also coached a team called the Ravensburg Towerstars, and under his father's watchful eyes and expertise, Leon skated with the team.

Leon also played for Jungadler Mannheim. During the 2011-2012 season, he scored 21 goals in the 35 games he played for the team. It was no surprise when he won the league's Player of the Year award.

During the 2012 CHL Import Draft, he was selected second overall by the Prince Albert Raiders of the Western Hockey League (WHL). He played here for a few years before he was traded to the Kelowna Rockets during the World Junior Championship.

The Rockets made it to the 2015 WHL championship game. Although they didn't win the cup, Leon was exceptional and named most valuable player. He also won the Stafford Smythe Trophy as Memorial Cup MVP.

Leon was creating ripples in the hockey world. He was drafted in the 2014 NHL Entry Draft and taken as the third overall player that year. The Edmonton Oilers signed him, making him the highest-drafted German-trained player in NHL history. Straight out of training camp, he found his way onto the opening night roster, and in October of 2014 Leon scored his first of many NHL goals.

Leon was now on a team with Connor McDavid—and one where the great Wayne Gretzky had previously played. But he wasn't starstruck by anyone. He was there to play, and that's what he did. His determination and consistency in scoring goals saw him selected as the alternate captain for the 2019-2020 season, just before COVID-19.

The season was cut short due to the pandemic, but despite that fact, he was the best player on the team. He was given the Art Ross Trophy as the leading scorer for the year. Only two other Oilers had gotten that trophy—Wayne Gretzky and Connor McDavid. Leon became the third Oiler to receive the award, and the first German player to win it!

Leon also won other awards that season, like the Hart Memorial Trophy and the Ted Lindsay Award, for the league's most valuable player and most outstanding player, respectively. He also earned the nickname German Gretzky. Leon feels like he doesn't deserve to be compared to the Great One, but he has definitely lived up to the name.

In March 2017, Leon scored a hat trick in the playoffs against the Ducks. At 21 years of age, he became the youngest Oiler to score a playoff hat trick.

Leon is proud of his nationality and the fact that he has had the opportunity to play internationally for Germany. He played in the Junior World Championships in 2013 and 2014, and was team captain in 2014. He also played in the IIHF World Championships in 2014 and 2018.

His scoring ability is second only to Connor McDavid. In fact, he is the second-highest-ranked scorer for the Oilers. His eight-year contract with the team has also made him one of the biggest earners in the game.

Leon has achieved a lot in his career, but he isn't done yet. He has skated out of his father's shadow and shown that he is indeed worthy of the title German Gretzky. In the process, he has made both his father and his fatherland proud.

Leon understands that not everyone has the opportunities that he had while growing up. He wants every child to have access to hockey, no matter their nationality, and to make this happen, he has donated funds to several charities.

FUN FACTS ABOUT LEON DRAISAITL

1. Leon's father had over 20 years of experience playing professional ice hockey before becoming a hockey coach.
2. Leon is one of the biggest earners in the NHL.
3. He is referred to as the German Gretzky.
4. Leon's jersey number is 29. He has always worn this number.
5. His dog has its own Instagram account.

TRIVIA

1. What is Leon's jersey number?
2. Where was Leon born?
3. What nickname was given to Leon?
4. What position does Leon play for the Oilers?
5. What are the trophies Leon won in the 2019-2020 season, before COVID-19 struck?

INSPIRATIONAL FACTS ABOUT LEON DRAISAITL

1. Trophy Winner: Leon Draisaitl won the Hart Trophy as the NHL's Most Valuable Player in the 2019-2020 season.
2. Art Ross Trophy: He clinched the Art Ross Trophy for leading the NHL in points during the 2019-2020 season.
3. 50-Goal Season: Draisaitl achieved a 50-goal season during the 2018-2019 NHL season.
4. Ted Lindsay Award: He received the Ted Lindsay Award in 2020, recognizing him as the NHL's Outstanding Player as voted by his fellow players.
5. NHL First All-Star Team: Draisaitl was named to the NHL First All-Star Team in multiple seasons, solidifying his status as one of the league's top performers.

DAVID PASTRNAK

"Family, friends, and having fun"—these famous words are the mantra of famous Czech hockey player David Pastrnak.

David was born on May 25, 1996, and played a number of different sports when he was growing up. He played table tennis and ice hockey, and even did figure skating and rode a bike.

When he was three years old, he got his first pair of skates. They were too big for him, and they were for figure skating rather than ice hockey. Because his school didn't allow multiple sports, he eventually chose ice hockey, with the full support of his parents. His father's greatest dream was for David to play hockey professionally, but he told his son that the most important thing was to have fun.

David's mom also played a huge role in his success. Between sixth and ninth grade, she drove him to practice every day, even though it was at 6:00 am! She was happy to do this because she wanted her son to do what he loved to do.

David loved hockey, and he played every chance he got. When he would get home from school, he would drop his bag and head straight out to play.

Growing up, David played goalie, but he eventually had to give this position up because his family didn't have enough money to afford all of the equipment. Fortunately for the rest of us, he eventually moved to the position of winger—one that he has been amazing in.

In 2013, after years of battling cancer, his father died. This motivated David to train even harder so he could become an NHL player. The next year, his dream came true when he was drafted by the Boston Bruins in the 2014 NHL Entry Level Draft.

Of course, this meant that David would have to leave the Czech Republic to play in the NHL. When he told his mother that he would have to leave home and travel to Sweden, she was terrified at the idea of moving to a new country and having to learn a new language.

In addition to the new language, David found that life in Sweden was more expensive than life in the Czech Republic. He would eat pancakes for lunch and dinner because that was the cheapest thing to make. Groceries were expensive, and so were other bills he had to pay, but he made it work.

After training camp, David played in the AHL for a while before starting his career in the NHL. He scored his first two goals in his first NHL game, when the Bruins played against the Philadelphia Flyers in January 2015.

We're sure his father would have been so proud to see his son finally playing in the NHL and scoring two goals in his first appearance! The Bruins won that game with three goals, and people immediately took interest in David.

In March 2015, the Bruins played against the Carolina Hurricanes and won. During that game, David became the youngest player on the team to score an overtime, game-winning goal in the regular season! He became very popular in Boston, and was given the nickname "Pasta."

During a game against the Penguins in the 2015-2016 season, David became the youngest Bruins player to score a penalty shot. His achievements just kept stacking up!

David continued to make his family proud on the ice. In October 2019, he scored four goals in a win over the Anaheim Ducks, becoming the 25th player in Bruins history to score four goals in a single game! Later that season, he won the Maurice "Rocket" Richard Trophy. No Bruin had ever won that award, but David changed that when he scored 48 goals in a season, tying Alexander Ovechkin of the Washington Capitals for most goals in the NHL.

Even though he had to leave home to play in the NHL, David never forgot where he came from. He played with his national team at the 2013 Ivan Hlinka Memorial Tournament, where he won a bronze medal. He also won a silver medal at the 2014 IIHL World U18 Championships.

David is a fun guy to be around with. He loves playing hockey, and he believes that playing has to be fun. The three most important things to him are family, friends, and fun. These are three Fs that we can all learn from.

FUN FACTS ABOUT DAVID PASTRNAK

1. David was born in the Czech Republic.
2. He played table tennis and soccer when he was younger.
3. David had pancakes for lunch and dinner every day for a month when he first moved to Sweden.
4. David's father also played hockey, but he didn't force his son to play. David just grew to love the sport on his own.
5. David's jersey number is 88, and he plays the position of right winger for the Boston Bruins.

TRIVIA

1. Why did David have to leave the Czech Republic?
2. In what championship did David win a bronze medal?
3. David was the first Bruin to achieve what?
4. What happened to David's father?
5. What principle does David live by today?

INSPIRATIONAL FACTS ABOUT DAVID PASTRNAK

1. Rocket Richard Trophy: David Pastrnak won the Maurice "Rocket" Richard Trophy for leading the NHL in goals during the 2019-2020 season.
2. Youngest Bruins Player to Score 50 Goals: Pastrnak became the youngest player in Boston Bruins history to score 50 goals in a single season during the 2019-2020 NHL season.
3. He wasn't discouraged even when he had to eat pancakes for lunch and dinner
4. Stanley Cup Final Appearance: Pastrnak played a key role in helping the Boston Bruins reach the Stanley Cup Final in the 2018-2019 season.

5. Philanthropic Initiatives: Pastrnak is involved in various philanthropic activities, demonstrating his commitment to making a positive impact off the ice.

CALE MAKAR

Cale was born on October 30, 1998, in Canada, the home of hockey. He was named after Cale Hulse, a former NHL player. This should have been the first sign that he would one day play hockey.

Cale received a pair of hockey sticks as his first Christmas gift. He would grip the sticks in his tiny hands and walk around the house. He wasn't even two years old yet, but he loved his mini-sticks so much that when his family went on vacation in Hawaii, his father packed them so that Cale would have something to play with. He would wake up excited to play with his hockey sticks on the beach every morning.

After Cale's adventure at the beach, his parents knew that he needed somewhere to play hockey—some place safe, where he wouldn't destroy anything in the house. To that end, the extra family room was transformed into a makeshift hockey room. It had a hockey net, balls instead of pucks, and an old carpet that Cale would painstakingly vacuum in a particular pattern.

Cale's love for hockey was fueled by his father and his cousin, both of whom played. His younger brother also played hockey. It was truly a family sport!

Cale spent some time in a minor hockey program called the Crowchild Blackhawks before moving on to the Northwest Calgary Athletic Association (NWCAA). He played at the Bantam level in 2011. He then played for the Calgary Flames in the 2014-1015 season. That year, he led the team in scoring and was named MVP. Because of this achievement, he was selected to the Alberta Midget Hockey League's first All-Star Team.

He then joined the Brooks Bandits, but while he was with the team he went through a painful experience. Normally, his father and mother were always there to cheer him on in every hockey game he played, but his father got ill and was hospitalized. He even had to be hooked up to oxygen machines in the hospital.

Even though he was ill, Cale's father still wanted to watch his son play. He was wheeled into the game with his oxygen tanks for Cale's playoff game. This moment was extremely touching and memorable for Cale and his family, because his father passed away a month later.

This kind of loss can send anyone into a spiral of depression, but not Cale. He rose up and decided to fight harder and do better on the ice. He would make his father proud!

By the time Cale was 17, he had earned the nickname "UMass hockey's crown jewel." In his first season, he helped the Bandits win the Alberta Junior Hockey League (AJHL). He received the AJHL and CJHL Rookie of the Year awards, the Western Canada Cup Top Defenseman award, and the RBC Top Defenseman, Top Scorer, and Most Valuable Player awards.

During college, Cale decided to continue with the UMass Minuteman program. The program was in serious need of rebuilding, but Cale knew that was where he was needed. He turned the program around and finished ninth in defenseman scoring in the Hockey East. He was also selected to the All-Rookie Team and his third All-Star Team.

In the 2018-2019 season, Cale led the team in scoring, and they finished second in the conference. He became the first Minutemen honored as the Hockey East Player of the Year, and he also won the Hobey Baker Award.

In April 2019, he signed with the Colorado Avalanche. He was the highest-drafted player from the AJHL, and fulfilled his childhood dream, scoring his first NHL goal against the Calgary Flames in the 2019 Stanley Cup playoffs.

Cale's journey to the NHL has been filled with ups and downs, but he has persevered. He celebrated with his teammates when they advanced to the finals of the 2022 Stanley Cup Playoffs, where they eventually won. For his performance, Cale was referred to as the "best player in the league" and awarded the Conn Smythe Trophy as most valuable player.

Just as importantly, Cale is active in giving back to his community. He took the Stanley Cup to the Crowchild Twin Arena for the kids to see. They were all excited to see the famous trophy, as well as their hero, Cale Makar.

FUN FACTS ABOUT CALE MAKAR

1. Cale's favorite color and scent is lemon.
2. His cousin and younger brother also play in the NHL.
3. Cale's nickname on the Colorado Avalanche is "Cale Salad."
4. His favorite old movie is *Back to the Future*.
5. Cale compared himself to Dash in *The Incredibles* because he is so fast.

TRIVIA

1. Where was Cale's first hockey rink?
2. Who was Cale named after?
3. When he was 10 years old, Cale wanted to become a _____ and a _____.
4. What did Cale do on the beach in Hawaii?
5. What position does Cale play for the Avalanche?

INSPIRATIONAL FACTS ABOUT CALE MAKAR

1. He knew that he needed good grades and skills to be successful.
2. He played hockey whenever he had the chance, even on a hot Hawaiian beach.
3. Cale knows how much children needs inspiration, which is why he took the Stanley Cup to the Crowchild Twin Arena.
4. He was able to quickly rise to the NHL because of his remarkable skills as a defenseman.
5. Cale is known for his work ethic, skills, and humility. He is a role model to many people in the hockey world.

MATTHEW TKACHUK

Matthew Tkachuk was born into a family of hockey. Not only did his father play, but he did so in the NHL!

Matthew was born in Arizona on December 11, 1997, and pretty much grew up on an ice rink. There are countless pictures of Matthew and his brothers in the arms of NHL stars like Gordie Howe and Patrick Kane.

When asked about his childhood in Arizona, Matthew's response was, "I'm sure that's where I first started to love the game." He loved hockey so much that his mother would drop him off at the ice rink where his dad was practicing, and he would hang out with the team's equipment managers. His father played for the Phoenix Coyotes, and young Matthew would wear the team's uniform and run around with his mini-sticks.

Matthew was just three when his father was transferred to the St. Louis Blues, and the entire family had to move with him. He and his brothers met all of their father's teammates, who would often stay over at their house. They also went to all of their father's games, and even the 2006 Winter Olympics.

Matthew's childhood and teenage years were filled with learning from his father and his father's teammates. He learned from the best, and absorbed as much as he could. He also collected keepsakes. Anytime he and his brothers met a new hockey player, their mom would take pictures. Some of Matthew's most prized possessions include pictures with Sidney Crosby, Alex Ovechkin, and Evgeni Malkin.

Matthew kept all his keepsakes and pictures on his bedroom walls in their home in St. Louis, but when it was time to move again, his mom came up with a better solution: a photo album. In addition to his book of photos, he had signed jerseys in his room from Tom Brady, Alex Ovechkin, and Sidney Crosby.

Just because he traveled with his father didn't mean he didn't have a proper education. Matthew attended Oak Hill School and Chaminade College Preparatory School. At the same time, he played hockey with the youth affiliate of his father's team, the St. Louis Blues. His team competed in the 2010 Quebec International Pee-Wee Hockey Tournament, and a few years later he was drafted by the London Knights in the Ontario Hockey League (OHL).

Matthew also played two seasons with the USA Hockey National Team Development Program. He played for the US National U17 Team (USDP), where he won his first gold medal; and the US National U18 Team (USDP), where he won his second gold medal. In his second season with the USDP, he finished second on the team after he scored 38 goals in 65 games.

Matthew followed his father's footsteps when he was selected by the Calgary Flames in the 2016 NHL Entry Level Draft, and soon scored his first NHL goal against the Buffalo Sabres. But on March 20, 2017, Matthew was benched for two games. In a game against the Los Angeles Kings, he hit Drew Doughty in the face with his elbow. It might have been a mistake, but rules are rules, and he had to pay the consequences.

Matthew took this in stride, and when he was allowed back on the ice he gave his all. He ended up finishing seventh for the Calder Memorial Trophy. Although he had two more suspensions, he was eventually named an alternate captain for the Flames in the 2018-2019 season.

After a few seasons with the Flames, Matthew was traded to the Florida Panthers. In his first season with his new team, Matthew broke the record for points in a season with 109. In addition, he was a finalist for the Hart Memorial Trophy.

In 2023, the race to the Stanley Cup was a tough one, but he played well and led the Panthers to the finals after scoring four goals against the Carolina Hurricanes.

One of the many things he learned from his parents while growing up was to make memories and always open your home to teammates. In fact, Matthew once invited the team's supporting staff, trainers, doctors, and a few teammates to his house for dinner after a win. Not only is he a great player, but he's also a great person!

FUN FACTS ABOUT MATTHEW TKACHUK

1. Matthew's father, Keith Tkachuk, also played in the NHL.
2. He grew up around sports legends, and his mother has a picture album as a keepsake.
3. Matthew's younger brother also plays in the NHL, for the Ottawa Senators.
4. His younger sister also plays field hockey in school.
5. Matthew has played for two teams in the NHL.

TRIVIA

1. Where did Matthew's love for hockey begin?
2. Where was Matthew born?
3. What are a few of his keepsakes?
4. After playing with the Flames, Matthew was traded to what team?
5. How many gold medals does Matthew have, and where did he win them?

INSPIRATIONAL FACTS ABOUT MATTHEW TKACHUK

1. He was inspired to play hockey from watching his father play.
2. Matthew has keepsakes from many sports legends he met as a boy.
3. He already loved hockey when he was a young child.
4. Matthew learned how to be hospitable from his parents.
5. He values teamwork and isn't afraid to stand up for his teammates, both on and off the ice.

NATHAN MACKINNON

What does it take to be the first overall pick in the NHL? Lots of skills and practice—and Nathan MacKinnon has lots of both!

Nathan grew up in the same neighborhood as Sidney Crosby, although he was born eight years after Sidney, on September 1, 1995. He learned a lot from watching his neighbor, who just happened to be a hockey legend. Growing up in the Halifax suburb of Cole Harbour, they skated on the same ice rink and frozen pond, played in the same tournaments, and played ball hockey at the same tennis courts.

But Nathan had other inspirations, as well. His father ran marathons and played hockey as a goalie, and he had a great influence on his son when he was growing up. His father was also a fitness freak and a nutritionist. Nathan grew up eating the best food for fueling his body, and he maintains that diet today.

Nathan was fortunate to have the full support of his parents. His father skated with him on the ice and was always available to give him advice and skating lessons. And his mom was his biggest cheerleader. His parents were always available for him after all of his games, and whenever he needed someone to talk to.

As a child, Nathan played hockey in the minor ice hockey system in his neighborhood. Even then, he was exceptional. He was fast on the ice and scored goals in every game he played.

When he was 12, he played Bantam AAA for the Cole Harbour Red Wings, but after two seasons he decided it was time to leave home. He knew that he had to do so if he wanted to challenge himself and improve his skills, so Nathan followed in the footsteps of Sidney and went to boarding school at Shattuck-Saint Mary in Faribault, Minnesota.

Shattuck-Saint Mary had a reputation as having one of the best hockey programs. If you were planning on being a hockey player in the future, this was the boarding school you wanted to attend. Nathan had the opportunity to study and play ice hockey there, and he jumped at the chance.

Nathan was the second-youngest player in the under-16 Midget program at school, but he wasn't concerned about the fact that he was playing against older kids. He played so well that he got to represent Nova Scotia at the 2011 Canada Winter Games, where he scored eight goals. Although his team finished in seventh place, he was the fourth-ranked individual player.

During the 2011 Quebec Major Junior Hockey League (QMJHL) Draft, Nathan spent the day skating with the Omaha Lancers to clear his head while he waited for the draft news. He didn't have to wait long before the news came: He had been ranked as the best available player and selected first overall by Baie-Comeau Drakkar.

He didn't stay with the team long, as he was soon traded to the Halifax Mooseheads, where he scored many goals and led the team to their first Memorial Cup on May 26, 2013. He was also named MVP and earned a spot on the tournament All-Star Team.

In 2013, Nathan won the Ed Chynoweth Trophy and the Stafford Smythe Memorial Trophy. He led the Mooseheads to their first Memorial Cup win in May 2013, where he was named most valuable player and earned a spot on the tournament All-Star Team.

In the 2013 NHL Draft, Nathan was selected by the Colorado Avalanche as the first overall pick. He signed with the Avalanche on July 9, 2013. His first few games with the Avalanche were not that impressive, but as time went by, he began to get his bearings and went from being an average player to a great one. He worked hard and was finally getting the recognition he deserved as one of the top players in the NHL.

Nathan won the Calder Memorial Trophy as Rookie of the Year in 2014. He was the youngest player to win this trophy, and the third player in Avalanche history to do so. He was also selected to the NHL All-Rookie Team. In September 2020, he won the Lady Byng Memorial Trophy, which is awarded to the player who demonstrates good sportsmanship and gentlemanly conduct.

While Nathan is best known for the Stanley Cup that he won with the Avalanche in 2022, it is his sportsmanship and respectful demeanor that is most impressive. We should all aspire to be like Nathan—a great athlete and a great person.

FUN FACTS ABOUT NATHAN MACKINNON

1. Nathan loves hip hop and watches *The Breakfast Show* every morning on YouTube.
2. He is on a special diet and eats gluten-free meals.
3. Nathan and Sidney Crosby are neighbors today.
4. Nathan acted in a television show called *Mr. D*, where he played a fictionalized version of himself.
5. His nickname is "The Dog" because he loved the rapper Nate Dog so much as a teenager.

TRIVIA

1. Where was Nathan born?
2. Who was the hockey legend who grew up in the same neighborhood as Nathan?
3. What championship did Nathan win in 2022?
4. In the 2013 NHL Draft, Nathan was selected as the overall pick.
5. Nathan was born how many years after Sidney Crosby?

INSPIRATIONAL FACTS ABOUT NATHAN MACKINNON

1. He was inspired by Sidney Crosby, who grew up in his hometown.
2. He learned skating from his father.
3. His mom and sister were his biggest cheerleaders.
4. Through his hard work and resilience, Nathan has become one of the top players in the NHL.
5. Nathan leads his team by example. He serves as a role model to hockey players all around the world because of his leadership qualities and his reputation as a team player.

AUSTON MATTHEWS

Auston Matthews was born in San Francisco, California. Two months after his birth, his parents moved to Scottsdale, Arizona. Auston's mother is Mexican, and she taught him to speak Spanish.

Hockey is a cold-weather sport, but in Arizona the temperature can be near 100 degrees for most of the year. Fortunately, Auston didn't let the weather keep him from skating. That being said, he wasn't initially interested in hockey. When he was two years old, his parents would take him to watch the Phoenix Coyotes games, where the only interesting thing to Auston was the Zamboni machine that cleaned the ice.

As time passed, Auston developed an interest in the game, as well. The Coyotes created a passion in him, and, after his fifth birthday, he joined the Arizona Bobcats minor hockey program. He came from a family of athletes, so hockey came naturally to him. Auston's father played baseball at Loyola Marymount University in Los Angeles, and his uncle played in the NFL. When Auston began pursuing a professional career in hockey and found himself overwhelmed, he turned to his uncle for advice.

Auston worked on his stick handling and other skills on a small rink at a local hockey facility, and often played against boys who were older than him. When he was seven years old, he attended a skating camp hosted by Boris Dorozhenko, who had developed a skating and hockey skills program in Mexico. Auston learned a lot at the camp and impressed his father, who decided that he would keep working with Boris. Boris flew to America and lived with Auston's grandparents so he could train the boy.

Boris's techniques didn't involve pucks or hockey sticks. Instead, he taught Auston power skating and right-hand foot coordination. All of these lessons paid off for Auston, who is now considered one of the best young skaters in the NHL.

Auston played in the 2010 Quebec International Pee-Wee Hockey Tournament with the Kharkiv minor ice hockey team. In 2012, he was selected by the Everett Silvertips in the Western Hockey League (WHL) to play for the USA Hockey National Team Development Program. That season, he played for the US National Team (USDP), and his skills on the ice drew the attention of NHL scouts.

In 2015, Auston won the USA Hockey Bob Johnson Award. This award is given for excellence in international competition, where Auston had a total of 116 points, breaking the previous record. He played two more seasons with the USDP and was named the most valuable player at the 2015 World U18 Championships. He was also the top scorer.

Auston was ready for the NHL, but he missed the 2015 draft age qualification by two days. Since he couldn't participate in the draft, he decided to join the ZSC Lions and play in the Swiss National League (NLA) for a year. He was the second-highest scorer with the Lions and won the NLA Rising Star Award.

It was probably good that Auston had to wait for the 2016 NHL Draft, because by then there was no debate at all—he was the first overall pick and signed with the Toronto Maple Leafs.

He made his NHL debut in a match against the Ottawa Senators, scoring four goals in the game. He was the first player in modern NHL history to score four goals in his debut!

In January 2017, he was the only Leafs player selected to participate in the 2017 NHL All-Star Game. He scored 67 points and broke the franchise record for most points in a season. He also finished the season with 40 goals, finishing second in number of goals for the NHL that season. Auston was awarded the Calder Memorial Trophy as the NHL's top rookie, becoming the first Leafs rookie to receive the trophy in 50 years!

In 2019, Auston renewed his commitment to the Toronto Maple Leafs by signing a five-year contract. He was also named to the NHL All-Star Team for three consecutive years.

The 2020-2021 season was shortened by the COVID-19 pandemic. Despite this fact, it was one of Auston's most successful seasons. He even won the Maurice "Rocket" Richard Trophy for most goals in a regular season.

Auston suffered a wrist injury in the 2021-2022 season and had to miss six weeks of training and the first three games of the year. But it ended up being an amazing season for the Toronto Maple Leafs, and for Auston. He made his mark in the NHL as one of the league's top scorers and was selected to play in the NHL All-Star Game for the fourth time.

He missed another three weeks in the 2022-2023 season due to a knee injury, but, upon returning to the ice, he quickly caught up and became one of seven players in the NHL to record 15 shots in a single game.

Auston has come a long way from the tiny ice rinks he practiced on when he was a child. He is now known as one of the top players and scorers in the NHL. The best part is that he is in his prime, and nowhere close to done. He is still scoring and winning with the Toronto Maple Leafs, and will likely be doing so for a few more years.

FUN FACTS AUSTON MATTHEWS

1. Auston speaks Spanish.
2. He has a massive tattoo of a Lion wearing a crown across his shoulder and down to his elbow.
3. Auston's agent is Pat Brisson.
4. His nickname is "Papi."
5. Some of Auston's favorite clothing brands are Gucci, Off-White, Givenchy, and Louis Vuitton.

TRIVIA

1. What city was Auston born?
2. What sport did Auston's father play in college?
3. What animal did Auston tattoo on his body?
4. Who was Boris Dorozhenko, and how did he and Auston meet?

WHAT TEAM DOES AUSTON PLAY FOR IN THE NHL?

INSPIRATIONAL FACTS ABOUT AUSTON MATTHEWS

1. He was so dedicated to learning that his parents paid for a coach to train him.
2. He was very interested in learning new techniques, even ones that didn't involve a puck.
3. He learned how to pass and skate on tiny ice rinks.
4. Even though Arizona was hot most of the year, he didn't let that stop him from skating.
5. He knows the meaning of teamwork, and works with his teammates to ensure they give their best in every game.

CONNOR MCDAVID

Connor McDavid was born in Richmond Hill, Ontario, on January 13, 1997. He grew up in the land of ice, where hockey lives in the heart of virtually everyone. Many children born in Canada are passionate about becoming hockey players when they grow up.

Connor's parents also played hockey. His mother played one year of recreational ice hockey as a child before she chose to ski, and his father played hockey in high school. Drawing on his experience, he played a huge role in teaching hockey to his son.

Connor's mother wanted him to ski—she loved the sport and wanted to share it with him. The boy was introduced to skiing as soon as he could walk, but when he got into hockey at age three, that became his main focus. His parents fully supported his decision to play hockey, and the family basement was converted into a venue for Connor to practice. Nets were placed at either end of the basement to resemble a real ice rink, and Connor would put on his rollerblades and shoot pucks at the nets. His goalkeepers were his mom or grandmother, and the fans around the rink were his favorite stuffed animals.

When his mother was tired of playing goalie, she would return to her chores. Soon, she'd hear Connor shouting from the basement, "I just scored the winning goal in the Stanley Cup Finals." The precocious three-year-old was already imagining himself playing for the Stanley Cup finals.

When he was four years old, Connor began to play hockey with a team. His parents even lied about young Connor's age, telling the coach he was five years old so he could play with the other kids.

Although his teammates were older than him, Connor was obviously more skilled than the rest. But when he was six years old, the local hockey association in his hometown banned Connor from playing against older kids. Apparently, a lot of parents didn't like the idea of Connor playing better than their children.

Connor quickly got bored, so his parents enrolled him in a hockey program in Aurora, Ontario. His father also bought him a Leafs jersey, because Connor was a big fan of the Maple Leafs. He attended their games and cheered for them, and when his father bought him the jersey, the number 97 was printed on the back. This number represented the year he was born, and it's the number Connor has stuck with over the years.

In the Ontario hockey program, he played with the York Simcoe Express. His father coached the team, and Connor demonstrated what a skilled player he was on the ice. He won four championships with the team.

Connor was the best junior hockey player in the area, and eventually left his father's team to play for the Toronto Marlboros of the Greater Toronto Hockey League. Not only did he win the GTHL Player of the Year Award, he also received the Tim Adams Memorial Trophy as the most valuable player.

His parents drove him and his brother to all of their games, and during the long rides, they would play music and talk. Connor is a pretty private person, so the person he turned to the most whenever he needed to talk was his mother. She began to see that her son's pretend games when he was younger could actually become a reality, and was happy that Connor was doing what he loved.

Connor was granted an exceptional player status through Hockey Canada and allowed to enter the junior hockey draft at the age of 15, rather than the normal age of 16. Once again, he was back to playing with people who were older than him. He was the first overall selection in the OHL draft that year, and picked by the Erie Otters. He also won the 2012 Jack Ferguson Award.

By the time Connor was 14, NHL scouts had already started watching him. When the 2015 NHL Draft came around, it was unsurprising when Connor was picked by the Edmonton Oilers with their first overall pick.

In November 2016, Connor scored his first NHL hat trick against the Dallas Stars. The following month, he scored his first shootout goal in a win over the Tampa Bay Lightning. He also became the first player to reach 50 points during the 2016-2017 season.

In April 2019, Connor had an accident in the final game of the Oilers' season, slamming his left knee against the opposing team's post while skating fast. He refused to undergo surgery to operate on the tears in his muscle and ligament, and instead chose conservative rehabilitation. He wanted to be able to return to play for the 2019-2020 season, and recovering from a surgery would not permit that.

Connor ended up recovering in time, and was able to start the season with the Oilers. That year, he reached Sidney Crosby's milestone of 400 NHL points in 306 games.

Connor became captain of the Oilers at the age of 19 years and 286 days, making him the youngest captain in the history of the NHL. Throughout his career, he has also achieved many awards, including the Ted Lindsay Award, the Hart Memorial Trophy, and three Art Ross Trophies. He is also known as one of the fastest skaters in the NHL. He also won the NHL All-Star Game's Fastest Skater competition amongst other achievements.

FUN FACTS ABOUT CONNOR MCDAVID

1. Connor has worn the number 97 on his jersey since he was a little boy.
2. He has a sweet tooth, and one of his favorite treats is black licorice.
3. Connor has a miniature Bernedoodle named "Lenny."
4. He is a big of the Toronto Maple Leafs, and has been since he was a young boy.
5. Connor's favorite player is Sidney Crosby.

TRIVIA

1. Where was Connor born?
2. What team does Connor play for today?
3. In what year's NHL draft was Connor picked by the Oilers?
4. Who played as his goalkeeper in the basement rink when Connor was three years old?
5. Connor was the youngest hockey player in NHL history.

INSPIRATIONAL FACTS ABOUT CONNOR MCDAVID

1. Connor is known as one of the most talented player in the NHL and has been compared with hockey legends like Wayne Gretzky and Sidney Crosby.
2. Connor dreamed big when he was young, and didn't let anything stop him from achieving his goals.
3. He was so good at hockey that he played with kids who were older.
4. He was named captain of the Oilers when he was just 19 years old, demonstrating great leadership skills, both on and off the ice.

5. Connor is known for being generous. He gives to various charities to help make a positive impact in others' lives.

CONCLUSION

Now that you have read the stories of your hockey heroes, we hope you have been inspired to do your best! These legends skated faster, scored more goals, stopped more goals, and played harder than anyone else, but they were only able to do so because they put in the time and hard work. They all came from different backgrounds and had different childhood experiences, but they have one thing in common—they all play with passion!

Here's a little cheer to encourage you during challenging time:

Don't ever give up on your dreams

Work hard in anything you do

Don't forget, the sky is the limit

Dream big and be different!

BONUS SECTION AFFIRMATIONS TO HELP YOUNG ATHLETES IMPROVE CONFIDENCE AND THEIR MENTAL GAME

MENTAL MINDSET FOR YOUNG ATHLETES

Hockey, a fast-paced sport played on ice, with two teams using sticks to maneuver a puck into the opponent's goal, is popular in many countries, with variations like ice hockey, field hockey, etc. Matches typically consist of three periods, each lasting for about 20 minutes. It is known for its physicality, skill, and mental competition.

For this piece, we'll discuss the mental mindset of young athletes who are into the hockey game and how young athletes can improve on the mental side of hockey. A mental mindset for an athlete refers to the established pattern of thinking that influences how an athlete perceives, interprets, and responds to various situations and challenges. It encompasses attitudes, beliefs, emotions, and thought processes that shape behavior and decision-making. A positive mental mindset often involves resilience, optimism, determination, and adaptability. In contrast, a negative mindset may involve pessimism, self-doubt, and fear of failure. Developing a strong mental mindset for an athlete is essential for achieving goals, overcoming obstacles, recovering from injury, and thriving in different aspects of life.

IMPORTANCE OF MENTAL STRENGTH IN HOCKEY

Let's quickly introduce you to the importance of gaining mental strength when it comes to hockey sport. Hockey is more than just a physical sport played on ice; it's also a mental game. While mastering skills like skating, shooting, and passing are essential, having mental strength is equally important for success on the ice. In hockey, maintaining focus, staying composed under pressure, and bouncing back from setbacks can often be the difference between winning and losing.

We will also explore the significance of mental strength in hockey and how young athletes can develop and improve it, from building confidence and resilience to enhancing concentration and mastering mental toughness to various aspects of the mental game and provide practical strategies for young hockey players to thrive both on and off the ice.

Being a beginner in hockey is totally alright you just need to cultivate mental strength which will enhance your performance and overall success.

MENTAL CHALLENGES YOUNG ATHLETES FACE

Like other sports, hockey athletes encounter many mental issues that can affect their performance and overall well-being. From managing expectations and dealing with pressure to coping with setbacks and scaling through the ups and downs of a demanding sport, the mental aspect of hockey can be challenging for players of all levels. Here, we'll look at some of the common mental challenges young athletes face and discuss strategies for overcoming them:

1. Fear of Failure

This is a common mental challenge that young athletes encounter. The fear of making mistakes, losing games, or not living up to expectations can lead to self-doubt and hesitation on the ice. Overcoming the fear of failure requires developing resilience and a growth mindset, where mistakes are viewed as opportunities for learning and growth rather than sources of shame or disappointment. Moreover, it is commonly said that you attract what you focus on; this is the psychology behind the fear of failure, which makes one consciously or subconsciously focus on failure. This is why athletes must remain steadfast in being positively minded so that even when there's a disappointment, it will quickly be seen as an opportunity.

2. Performance Anxiety

Another common mental challenge young hockey players face is performance anxiety. Whether it's the pressure to perform well in a game, the fear of letting down teammates and coaches, or the anxiety of facing a tough opponent, performance anxiety can negatively affect confidence and hinder performance. Learning to manage and cope with performance anxiety is crucial for young athletes to unlock their full potential.

3. Balancing School and Hockey

For many young athletes, balancing academic responsibilities with the demands of hockey can be a significant source of stress and pressure. Juggling schoolwork, homework, training, and games can leave little time for relaxation and downtime, leading to burnout and exhaustion. Finding a healthy balance between school and hockey is crucial for maintaining mental well-being and overall success on and off the ice. It is important to emphasize finding this balance, this is because when one of these two (school or hockey) is adversely affected, it can lead to serious mental issues like depression, but don't worry of our hockey heroes could balance this, you can do it too.

4. Managing Expectations

The pressure to meet expectations from coaches, parents, fans, teammates, and oneself can create immense mental stress for young athletes. Striking a balance between striving for excellence and maintaining realistic expectations is essential for preserving mental well-being and enjoying the sport of hockey. Setting personal goals, focusing on improvement, and embracing the process rather than solely the outcome can help alleviate the pressure of external expectations. Likewise, athletes must let coaches, parents, fans, and teammates understand that they are human and not omnipotent. This is to make everyone understand that athletes are neither perfect nor infallible. Hence, they are not pressured to keep up with a particular lifestyle or meet unnecessary expectations.

5. Dealing with Setbacks

Setbacks are inevitable in hockey, whether it's a loss, an injury, or a slump in performance. How young athletes respond to setbacks can greatly impact their mental resilience and long-term development in the sport. Learning to bounce back from setbacks, stay positive, and persevere through adversity is a valuable skill that young athletes can cultivate through experience and support from coaches and mentors.

Mental challenges are an inbuilt part of the journey for young hockey players. Still, they also present opportunities for growth, resilience, and personal development. By acknowledging and addressing these challenges head-on, young athletes can develop the mental strength and resilience that is needed to thrive in hockey and beyond.

HOW TO IMPROVE YOUR MENTAL HEALTH AS A YOUNG ATHLETE

1. **Focus:** Players must stay focused during games and practices, concentrating on the task and blocking distractions.
2. **Resilience:** Resilience encourages players to bounce back from setbacks, such as losses or mistakes, by focusing on improvement. Setbacks and failures are inevitable in hockey, but they also present opportunities for growth and learning. Encourage young athletes to embrace adversity as a natural part of the journey and to approach challenges with a resilient mindset. Help players reframe setbacks as opportunities for learning and improvement and support them in returning stronger than before. Foster a team culture that celebrates resilience and perseverance and provides encouragement and support during difficult times.
3. **Confidence:** Players build confidence in their abilities through practice, constructive feedback, and celebrating successes, no matter how small. Focusing on strengths is also key to building confidence.
4. **Positive Affirmations:** How young athletes talk to themselves can significantly impact their confidence and performance. Players must be encouraged to replace negative self-talk with positive affirmations and self-encouragement. Remind players to focus on their strengths, past successes, and progress rather than dwelling on mistakes or shortcomings. By cultivating a positive internal dialogue, players can boost confidence, resilience, and self-belief on the ice.

5. **Mindfulness:** Mindfulness techniques help players stay present (both physically and psychologically) and manage stress during games and practices.
6. **Handling Pressure:** Teach young athletes how to manage pressure and perform under stressful situations. This includes staying calm, focusing on the present moment, and trusting their abilities.
7. **Sportsmanship:** Emphasize the importance of good sportsmanship, including respect for teammates, opponents, coaches, and officials. Encourage fair play and integrity both on and off the field.
8. **Goal Setting:** Setting clear, achievable goals is essential for maintaining motivation and tracking progress in hockey. Young athletes should set short-term and long-term goals for skill development, performance improvement, and team success. Utilize the SMART goal-setting framework (Specific, Measurable, Achievable, Relevant, Time-bound) to ensure clear and attainable goals. Players should create action plans outlining the steps they need to take to achieve their goals and provide support and guidance.
9. **Adaptability:** Teach players to easily adapt to changing situations on the ice, whether adjusting to different opponents, strategies, game or weather conditions.
10. **Teamwork:** Emphasize the importance of teamwork and communication, helping players understand their roles and how to support their teammates.
11. **Enjoyment:** Above all, remind players to have fun and enjoy the game, fostering a love for hockey that will keep them motivated and engaged for years to come.

Building mental strength is a continual process that requires dedication, practice, and support. By incorporating these practical strategies and techniques into their training and competition routines, young hockey players can develop the resilience, confidence, and focus needed to succeed on the ice and beyond. Additionally, hockey players must understand that life outside the ice completely differs from that on the ice. Players must know that whatever happens outside the ice stays outside the ice. Understanding this as a fact helps players avoid mixing personal life happenings with the hockey career they are building. As stated in the points mentioned above, a key point to build a strong mental foundation involves making a reasonable separation between players' personal life and their lives as a hockey player.

HUNDRED AFFIRMATIONS FOR CHILDREN

1. I am not easily discouraged.
2. I am strong and able to do whatever I put my mind on.
3. I turn every disadvantage into my advantage.
4. I am the Wayne Gretzky of my hockey team.
5. I surpass my trainers' and coach's expectations of me.
6. I am a game-changer.
7. I am unstoppable on the ice.
8. My skating techniques are topnotch.
9. I break records in every game I play.
10. I love new challenges on the ice.
11. Ice hockey blood flows in my veins
12. I am capable of great things.
13. I am a good teammate both on and off the ice.
14. I inspire and motivate my teammates.
15. I always stand out in any position I play on my team.
16. Learning is my passion and I always aim to be better.
17. My body is a well-oiled machine, no rusting, no resting till we are the best out here!
18. I am not scared of hard work.
19. I will never look down on my teammates.
20. Everyday is an opportunity to learn something new.
21. I will treat my coaches and teammates with respect
22. I believe in myself and my hockey stick!
23. I can jump high because I am not scared of new heights!
24. I will reach my full athletic potential.
25. I can perform well in any competition.

26. I have full stamina on the ice.
27. Keep moving forward, never backward.
28. I will stick to my position and give it my all.
29. The sky is the limit for me.
30. I am disciplined and focused.
31. I am not moved by the tides and waves around me.
32. I am confident that I will win.
33. I am confident that I will always win and will always keep winning.
34. I am excited to learn new things, skills and techniques that can make me better.
35. I love hockey and I have fun while playing it.
36. The size of the rink doesn't matter, what matters is how I play.
37. I will always dream big because the sky is my limit!
38. I am relentless.
39. I am proud of my efforts.
40. I am strong and resilient.
41. I will dream big and believe I can achieve them.
42. I am amazing and I do amazing things.
43. I am getting better in my skills and techniques every day.
44. I am surrounded by positive energy.
45. I am grateful for every little thing I have.
46. I've got the best supporters in the world.
47. I can solve any problem that comes my way.
48. I follow advice and listen to instructions.
49. I am always open to new ideas.
50. Learning is fun and exciting.
51. I can face any hurdle that comes my way.
52. When I fall, I rise back up
53. I've got the strength to carry on till the end of the finish line.
54. It's okay to ask questions.
55. I'm getting smarter every day.
56. I am a good leader like Connor McDavid.

57. I have a big heart and I always read to help those in need.
58. I will always be kind.
59. I am always patient with others.
60. I'm becoming stronger day by day.
61. I use kind words to people around me.
62. I am positive no matter the wins and losses.
63. I am full of potential and possibilities.
64. I am a source of inspiration to others.
65. I motivate others around me.
66. I am truthful and honest in everything I do.
67. I do not lose my cool even when my team loses.
68. I face my fears and I overcome them.
69. Being sweaty is worth it.
70. I am dedicated to my training
71. I am purposeful and driven.
72. I know I was born with limitless potential.
73. I never give up in the face of any challenge.
74. My endurance is very high.
75. I stay focused even under pressure.
76. I enjoy training and practicing.
77. I skate faster on the ice.
78. The aches that I feel are rewarding
79. I am born to be an ice champion.
80. I love challenging competitions.
81. I am mentally strong in any situation.
82. My mental health is on a hundred percent.
83. I always win in any game I play.
84. I have total trust in my abilities.
85. I am confident because I am winning this
86. I am brave enough to try new things.
87. I am helpful and full of compassion.
88. I am strong physically, emotionally, and mentally.
89. I am perfect just the way I am.

90. Giving up is not in my DNA.
91. I'm an ice champion.
92. I am an upcoming legend.
93. I am faster than a bullet.
94. I am as fast as a cheater and as graceful as a swan.
95. My coordination on the ice rink is flawless.
96. My comeback is like a Phoenix rising from the ashes.
97. I am a force to be reckoned with on the ice.
98. I will reach my full athletic potential.
99. I am a sports prodigy.
100. I am among the best of the best in the ice hockey game.